Motivating the Disaffected

Motivational Triggers

Dr Gerald Lombard

Motivational Triggers

Published by Lifetime Careers Wiltshire, 7 Ascot Court, White Horse Business Park, Trowbridge BA14 0XA.

ISBN 1 902876 67 9

Printed by Cromwell Press, Trowbrigde
Cover illustration by Russell Cobb
Text design by Ministry of Design

Motivating the Disaffected
Series editor: Dr Gerald Lombard

Motivational Triggers is one of a series of six titles designed to help professionals in education and advisory work to motivate and encourage students who are disengaged from learning.

Each book provides a concise and practical guide to topics that are of particular concern to teachers and advisers.

The other titles in the series are:

The ABC of Approach to Classroom Behaviour Management
Asperger Syndrome and high fuctioning autism:
      guidelines for education post 16
Social Competency: reading other people
Complex Specific Learning Difficulties
Staying Safe

To order copies, please contact Orca Book Services Ltd, Stanley House, 3 Fleets Lane, Poole, Dorset BH15 3AJ. Tel: 01202 665432. Fax: 01202 666219.

For further information about these and other products published by Lifetime Careers Publishing, please contact our customer services, tel: 01225 716023; email: sales@lifetime-publishing.co.uk, or www.lifetime-publishing.co.uk

Dr Gerald Lombard, C. Psychol., AFBPsS

Ged is Director of The Independent Psychological Service, which is an intervention and training service for young people and adults. He primarily works with individuals who 'won't, can't or can't be arsed' (one client's view of their work).

As a Chartered Psychologist, his major areas of interest are motivational principles, social competency (reading faces with intent) and complex specific learning difficulties. Ged was a secondary school teacher for 15 years, a part-time tutor/psychologist at two prisons and has held his current post for ten years.

Contents

Introduction

This publication is a brief overview of one approach used to help vulnerable and challenging individuals in training and education. Although this approach is based on psychological principles, it is hoped that 'psycho-babble' has been kept to a minimum.

The following is not intended to be a comprehensive guide to motivation in education and training. If readers find it a useful introductory guide, then a more detailed review of motivational principles and their application will follow. This first publication presents basic and tested fundamentals used to engage and motivate individuals.

Generally we know the profile type of the people who come to meet us in our service.

- They have a history of disaffection, or a difficulty in coping, with the education or training system they have found themselves in, or excluded from.

- They frequently experience relationship problems with many of their educators and trainers, and/or their peer group.

- They have deflated views of their abilities compared to others, which can occasionally present as inflated views of what they are capable.

- Their personal self-esteem is low, but can occasionally be masked by a higher social self-esteem if they are of a challenging sub-culture.

- Often there are family issues that are a significant part of their cycle of low achievement.

- Statutory organisations are, or have been involved, which have not helped in resolving the issues. This has often led to a distrust of authority, organisations or agencies that claim to help.

- Genuine specific problems with learning have frequently not been addressed or assessed, often leading to routes of study or training inappropriate to their learning style or cognitive strengths.

However, the principles we apply to those individuals with these types of profile are the same we present to motivated sixth formers, undergraduates, professional youth workers and colleagues. The only difference is the consistent application with explanations of why they are applied and what our expectations are (including boundaries).

We will begin by designing basic motivational principles without the research underpinning. However, for those who wish to follow up the ongoing research areas, Section 2 will provide a brief overview of 'New pointers from research on motivation'.

Section 1
The basics in motivation and its application

Addressing primary needs

Maslow (1968) believed that human beings are motivated by an intrinsic tendency called 'self-actualisation', i.e. a desire to develop their capacities to the full. Having worked with thousands of teenagers and adults I, too, believe this – it is their poor self-theories and circumstances that so often deny this. Indeed, I have never yet met a demotivated person: everyone I have met is highly motivated – but not always in areas I would like them to be, to help them to achieve their potential.

Despite Maslow's theory being almost 35 years old, I continue to apply it in my daily work – because without meeting an individual's primary motivating needs, all else is likely to be substantially weakened.

Diagram 1.1 simplifies Maslow's original model to serve its application with individual clients and groups.

Diagram 1.1: Simplistic application of Maslow

Willingness to take the risk

↑

Self-esteem

↑

Feeling included

↑

Feeling safe

↑

Meet physiological needs

In my daily practice, I will first meet the basic level of human motivation – food and drink. On a first meeting: *'Hello, I'm Ged. Would you like a cup of tea/coffee/water/orange?'* I do not offer high-sugar drinks, for reasons I will later explain. I also offer toast or biscuits. On subsequent meeting, it becomes a regular opening for a meeting: *'Cuppa?'* or *'Water?'* or *'Have a biscuit'.*

There are three key reasons for beginning this way:

1. Many of the clients I meet have not eaten or had a drink for many hours before I meet them. This is particularly likely if it is a morning meeting. Without food or drink, blood sugar is likely to be low. Further, if their diet is of a high carbohydrate and high sugar content (chips, fizzy drinks, chocolate, crisps), and/or alcohol or drug-oriented, they are likely to be dehydrated, irritable, lethargic and unresponsive. A 'shot' of tea/coffee/juice with a biscuit can help 'start them up'.

2. It is similar to the 'breaking of bread' – a signal that they are welcome.

3. It is beginning with offering something to another – and sharing: I will drink (and sometimes eat) with the client(s).

Often, there will be a refusal to accept the offer of a drink and a biscuit. This will be greeted with a smile from me, but water remains on offer and available. Individuals who are nervous or anxious often experience a dry-mouth sensation; add to this dehydration (75% of us are dehydrated at any one time) and this can increase irritability and distractibility. Many who refuse the original drink often pour themselves water during the meeting.

This basic guideline not only exists for clients but also professionals, and this is not only applicable to meetings. If individuals arrive for training (or clients for class) on a morning, hot drinks, water and biscuits (nut bars/fruit bars, too) are available. For afternoon training sessions water is available, with beverages mid-afternoon.

I celebrate breakfast clubs at schools, colleges and training centres. So often you hear how learning and attendance have improved since their introduction. A positive spin-off from these morning meals is the 'relationship effect'. This may be because families and living groups are less likely to eat together, and basic rules of etiquette are weakened, but more importantly social discourse between live-together groups are reduced. I have heard many training centres and schools reporting that since the introduction of breakfast clubs, peer confrontations have reduced, positive peer relationships have been enhanced, and manners have improved! In my experience, youth professionals in attendance are essential to promote this. Diet and behaviour will be examined further in Section 2.

Feeling safe

'Nothing is more despicable than respect based on fear' (Albert Camus). I see my main role as removing a sense of fear. Fear undermines creativity, undermines thought, freezes free spiritedness, and often takes away the freedom of 'taking the risk of getting it wrong'. These are key tenets of motivation. Therefore, when I introduce opportunities to vulnerable or challenging young people, I do not talk about them visiting centres, colleges or organisations – I talk about 'coming to play', i.e. play with ideas, play with equipment, play with people. Then, if you want to go back and find out more, do. I do not mention 'qualifications', 'outcomes', 'payment' – these are often demotivators to vulnerable or challenging individuals. However they can later become outcomes if the individual wants them to be. By removing fear-provoking outcomes, I find clients more willing to take the risk.

Other fears can relate to their peer group, the youth professional they are with, an individual in their training or teaching group, or a phobic reaction/ aggressive response to specific stimuli. Each of these should be considered, and if necessary addressed.

Fear of peer group can take two routes. The route of 'reputation theory' or 'fear of another'.

Reputation theory

This was discovered as a peer group influence by Nick Emler (University of Leeds). His research in the late 1990s (e.g. Emler and Reicher, 1995) found that many young people described as challenging, aimed to maintain or enhance the anti-establishment reputations they had gained. This would be accentuated when they were together or witnessed by other peers. To be caught by or escape from police, to appear in court, to be expelled from school – all would enhance reputations for individual acts that gained further respect from their peer group. Now many of these young people subsequently find themselves in Inclusion Units at schools (I remain in awe of the names attached to excluded groups), with Youth Offending Teams, on new impact/new start/new name schemes, or college courses from year 9. They attend these opportunities together. Often, they quickly attempt to demonstrate their reputation in another environment, because they have like-minded young people with reputations to maintain. Frequently, they compete and provoke behaviours to aim to increase their reputation over another.

To continue putting these groups of young people together throughout the day has been favoured policy – but the outcomes are so often disappointing.

Taking account of reputation theory is to acknowledge the powerful effect of peer influence, and the fear of losing 'street cool'. Therefore, attending an educational or training opportunity does not necessarily mean being placed in an environment to compete with reputations – by enabling young people to follow separate timetables, mixing with a variety of age groups, and in a variety of settings, with opportunities to discuss their concerns with a mentor. They can still meet their friends, but this is away from the learning or training environment, or at appointed breaktimes or tutorials (depending on how it best works for individuals in that setting).

In short, putting challenging young people together for extended periods of time is often doomed to fail – their old reputation agendas get in the way of gaining new reputations.

Fear of another

This can be of another peer, or a professional working with the individual. This cannot be ignored. One intimidatory individual can seriously inhibit learning. A popular intervention is to remove the young person intimidating others, provide some common-sense approaches and suggestions to the young person, then put them back in the same group – and subsequently complain that they were willing and co-operative individually, but worse when they returned to the original group. This should be a rapid decision-making process – does this person who provokes fear in this group need to be transferred to another group while support work is carried out for their problems with communication? To not address this problem can have significant effects on vulnerable members of the group. Note that I am emphasising fear – other irritating behaviours may be addressed while the individual remains within the group, but fear can uncouple successful work to date.

Feeling included

Once the primary needs of food and drink, temperature, lighting have been addressed, as well as feeling safe and secure, then feeling included and part of a group is an essential part of the motivational cycle. As Diagram 1.2 shows, when sight of this essential element is lost, then interconnections move along continuums in demotivating directions.

Diagram 1.2: The inclusion/exclusion continuum

INCLUSION	EXCLUSION	CONTROL	OPENNESS
↓	↓	↓	↓
FEELINGS	FEELINGS	FEELINGS	FEELINGS
↓	↓	↓	↓
LIKEABILITY	FEARS	FEARS	LIKEABILITY
	↓	↓	↓
	IGNORED	REJECTED	ACCEPTED
		↓	↓
		HUMILIATED	ACKNOWLEDGED

In other words, to feel included and experiencing some personal control over events and decisions in a spirit and atmosphere of openness, generates feelings of being liked and of liking others. However, the more the continuum moves away from feeling included, having personal control and exchange in an open atmosphere, the more it provides fears of being ignored, humiliated and rejected. Therefore, to generate positive motivation to 'want to do and be' requires the three elements of inclusion, control, and openness.

Therefore, our service's response is not to hide information or opinion. We will not 'embroider the doily', e.g.

> *'Yes, I know your reading is in the lowest 1% for your age but you are such a nice person.'*

We are more likely to say:

> *'Yes, your reading is not one of your strengths.'*

In response, clients are more open with us, expressing frustration and anger in words, not aggressive actions.

To make someone feel included requires basic warmth:

- a genuine, open smile with personal greeting: *'Hello, Ged'* (even after a previously tetchy day)

- an opportunity to talk together individually or in a small group before starting

- offer of food/drink

- a quiet acknowledgement of what they have brought with them today (a smile, a skateboard, a threat, a sad face).

If they arrive late, *not* to criticise but smile and greet, invite them in, and you will explain to them very soon what everyone else/you are doing. At the end of a session, *then* ask they why they were late while everyone is leaving, and follow it up with them if you need to.

Provide clear non-negotiable and negotiable rules and apply them to everyone. I have three *non-negotiable rules* for *everybody* (for both clients and professionals alike).

1. If you come to sessions (school, college, training) under the influence of alcohol or drugs you will go home. You are able to return in a week's time and re-negotiate your place. (A second occasion would result in losing their place and having to re-apply again one week later. A third occasion would mean final loss of place.)

2. If you threaten or attack anyone from your school/college/training group, you will go home. (The same applies as (1) above but a third occasion may not be an option if violence is involved.)

3. If you use racist or sexist language you will go home. (The same applies as in (1) above.)

The intention of three non-negotiables is that everyone has a clear guide of basics that are easy to remember – and they are seen to be applied immediately. It leaves everything else that occurs (e.g. swearing, rudeness) as negotiable – but the three non-negotiables are set in stone – for everybody, youth professionals included.

Recently, a 17-year-old student telephoned me to advise me he was on his way to meet me. He had obviously been drinking alcohol, made evident by the slurring of the occasional word, and my newly-acquired status of eternal brother to him. I interrupted only to say '*Turn round, go back home....*' and he finished the sentence, saying '*...and I can come back in a week?*'. Clear standards take away confrontation while letting the individual know that they are still included.

Only by taking basic elements into account is the individual likely to feel more secure in their *self-esteem*, and only then are they likely to take the risk to learn with you.

Finally, the value of helping young people with social communication skills remains underrated. We will examine the real need to include this in curricula and training schemes in another publication *Social Competency: reading other people*.

Motivational triggers

This approach is based on motivational research spanning 50 years. It works from the premise that young people's cognitions (thoughts) are dynamic and available for change. Therefore, to trigger students' cognitive styles positively may help to remotivate otherwise disaffected learners.

The aim with this approach is to trigger *intrinsic motivation*, i.e. doing something because you want to do it – the drive comes from within you. Unfortunately, much of our education system is based on *extrinsic motivation*, i.e. doing something because there is a reward or sanction that will follow (money, qualification, test outcome). Intrinsic motivation is more resilient and purposeful than extrinsic motivation. It is also more likely to provide a sense of fun and independent learning.

There is a sequence of motivational triggers that have been empirically researched (see Section 2) as promoting intrinsic motivation. They have been applied in education, training and sport. The sequence of triggers is:

- choice

- challenge

- curiosity

- competency

- information context

- fantasy

- promoting self-efficacy

- where is it leading, relevance, new challenges.

I apply these triggers in my daily work, both with clients and professionals.

Choice

I always try to make individuals feel they have a *choice*. It is important, however, to explain briefly both options you are giving. Giving three options is one too many. Here are some examples:

'You could come to college if you wish. If you come to college, you could try out plumbing/art and design/multi-media/construction etc. I'm OK about that. Or you could stay at school and continue with your GCSEs that you tell me you hate. I'm OK with that, too.'

'You could punch Steve if you want to. That is your choice. If you do you will lose your place here. If you don't punch Steve you will still have your place here while we find a way to sort this one out.'

'I'm OK that you don't do any work – the choice is yours. If you do your work you continue on the course, if you don't you will come off the course.'

'I do not have any problems with you not coming into work. If you do, you will get paid. If you don't, you won't get paid. The choice is yours.'

The key tenet of the *choice* trigger is the cognitive switch from your making someone do what you want them to do (external control) to your letting them choose with the consequence of each choice *briefly* explained. By so doing, you are not putting yourself into a blame situation – they have made their freewill choice with the accompanying consequences. We always avoid words such as 'have to', 'must' and 'need' because they reduce the feeling of personal control.

Challenge

Once a choice is made, I will provide a *challenge*. The client who is not sure about trying college will be given the opportunity to briefly but actively try multi-media, or plumbing, or design, etc. Talking about it should be brief. The challenge should be non-threatening and prepared. Sometimes, the challenge is enough to watch others at work. The client who is nervous visiting you can be given the *choice* of learning when they want, and the *challenge* of helping you with an activity (computer, setting up a piece of equipment) whilst you chat to them. A challenge should be practical, engaging and have a novel element to it. Again, it's not directing the individual to do a task but inviting them to engage in it. Clients who visit me will talk for a short time, and 'do' an activity for most of the time. Even asking someone to 'give you a hand' can introduce a challenge – but the challenge is for their interest, and not an opportunity for you to get them to put up your bookshelves!

Individuals entering a classroom could be met with a challenge – preferably visual and interactive. I occasionally use visual illusions, computer programs, or puzzles. It avoids the popular question, *'What rubbish are we doing today?'* They are already engaged in an activity, and talking about it.

Curiosity

Curiosity is an extension of challenge. Once individuals are interested, be aware of not giving all the jewels away at once, e.g. *'We can return to that one next time',* or end a session with a question to encourage research, or provoke by saying *'But we won't find that out until next time.'* If a young person refuses to some to see me from another room, I will use choice, challenge and curiosity when I speak to them:

> *'Hello – if you want to see me I'm two doors down the corridor. If you don't want to see me I'm OK with that. But if you don't come and see me you will never know what I was going to say to you.'*

The pulling power of human curiosity often helps me with individuals who claim they won't turn up – but they usually do.

Competency

Individuals who have lost faith in education or training often have a strong belief that you, too, will not be able to help them. Even if you provide them with an activity or task they can do, they often refuse to begin because of a belief that just around the corner you will show they are incompetent. I avoid this happening: I do not give individuals tasks they cannot do. I move from one task to another before their skill ceiling is reached. By so doing, I can return to an earlier completed task and raise the ceiling a little more again. It is a matter of building up their resilience slowly so when the going gets harder, they have an increased feeling of competency.

Information context

This is promoting information feedback on how someone is performing. Research with teenagers (Lombard, 1992) has demonstrated the importance of genuine feedback. Do try to avoid old, traditional words of praise, e.g. good or well done or excellent – these can have a deleterious effect on many demotivated, disaffected individuals. They often do not believe you, or find it false praise. One 15-year-old pupil told me that 'good' really means 'you are sat down, keeping quiet and not causing trouble and that must be good' – but it is not a comment on the standard of performance of a task.

Alternative, informational feedback should be more visual, e.g.:

- thumbs up

- a genuine smile (show them your face wrinkles!)

- a nod of the head

- a gentle tap on the table with a smile

- a previously agreed kinaesthetic signal, e.g. a light touch of the arm.

Once individuals understand your signals, they can begin to interpret the level of positive feedback. For example, one thumb from me means 'OK' but two thumbs and wide smile means 'brilliant'. Voice tone and voice volume should always remain calm and neutral – unless something funny or amusing or exciting is coming along, then volume and intonation can increase.

Information feedback can also help with behaviour guidance signals. These need to be negotiated and agreed with clients before they are used. I find them particularly useful for individuals who require frequent reminders in a group to stop talking, interrupting, or hindering others. The words 'Stop that' can provoke a group or become over used.

Signals I use with clients are:

- a light touch of the client's elbow and eye contact, which means 'stop what you are doing now'

- eye contact with the client and my fingers touching my eyebrow (like a salute) which means 'shut up' or 'you are talking too much – stop.'

Fantasy

Most of the clients I meet have not succeeded in school, and the majority tend to be visual or kinaesthetic thinkers. Their learning experiences have often been language based, i.e. taught from the front of a class in teacher-speak and writing their knowledge onto paper. However, many of the visual/kinaesthetic thinkers I meet experience literacy difficulties. This results in their being unable to demonstrate what they can do, or retain the information given to them.

Therefore, I use visual language when I speak, e.g. *'As black as coal', 'Light as a feather.'* I frequently tell stories while teaching. This is to stimulate visual imagery and access visual memory. My clients' auditory (spoken) memory is often very weak, so if I speak in pictures they are more likely to remember. My stories relate to what I am teaching: any sequences I teach will have a story. Anyone who has attended one of my courses will have been subjected to learning the planets with stories of the beautiful goddess Venus with ginger hair, blue flowing gowns and attractive perfumes, and the man putting up a fence with a big red face and a Mars Bar sticking out of his mouth. In other words, talking in pictures with a story that will recall the sequence of planets.

If an individual tells me they are interested in studying, for example, motor mechanics I will ask them, in their mind's eye, to open up the bonnet of a car. They tell me what they see (I will tell them it looks like spaghetti to me). If they were servicing the vehicle what would they look at first? What does it look like? Then what would they do?

Now if the aspiring motor mechanic is moving hands and eyes while talking, I can be reasonably assured they are visualising.

In other words, I promote visualising. It helps reduce tension (we can see this on biofeedback machines) and engenders more positive feelings. The best teachers (and comedians) generate pictures in the listener's head when talking.

Promoting self-efficacy

This trigger is promoting to the client 'you can do'. It is a daily reminder of what they have mastered. This is not intended to repeat the same thing each day – it may be a reference to how they supported a friend or peer, how their roller-blading was impressive, how much you enjoyed their company, or a comment about what they have achieved.

Where it is leading

I always explain the relevance to their lives – today, tomorrow and next year – in any work I do with a client. What we do with our clients has to be relevant to *their* daily lives, and their future. If what we do is not relevant to clients' lives *we should not be doing it*. For example, if I were teaching eye contact to young people, I would describe the different situations where they could gain advantage, e.g. chatting someone up, getting someone to trust you, appearing more or less threatening. If I were teaching numeracy, I would plan my course so it was directly relevant to what they are aiming to do, or the skills they want to improve. Only then, do they begin to see where it fits with them. If they cannot see the relevance, they will not engage. If they see the relevance, you can begin setting new challenges for where they want to go next.

Motivational triggers are essential to my daily practice. They have kept me safe and helped me motivate others. However, my practice is different to yours. If you try the triggers in your practice my advice is you develop your own delivery. More importantly, do not expect immediate positive results. These techniques are more effective over a period of time when clients perceive consistent management of their needs.

Motivational styles

Research on motivation in the 1980s and 1990s discovered two motivational styles particularly relevant to individuals with learning difficulties, behavioural difficulties, or both. However, it should be noted that we all display a particular style of motivation when we approach and involve ourselves in a task. The handicapping nature of two motivational styles are apparent when an individual becomes locked in either of the following:

- *learned helplessness,* originating from the work of Seligman (1975) and the extension of the theory to personal helplessness (Abramson, Seligman and Gardner, 1980)

- *self-worth concern*, originating from the work of Covington and Beery (1976), and later extended to high self-worth concern and threatened sense of self (Covington, 1984).

These two motivational styles have been empirically investigated (Craske, 1988; Galloway and Rodgers, 1989; Lombard, 1992) and the profiles are generally accepted as distinct entities, and are sometimes referred to as motivational deficits.

Learned helplessness and high self-worth concern require various considerations on the professional's behalf, to maintain or increase trainees' interest and motivation. The ultimate aim should be to achieve the most productive motivational style, called *self-determination*.

A brief description of each style will be followed by guidelines on how to manage motivational deficits.

Learned helplessness

This term derived from laboratory experiments with animals several decades ago. There was evidence that animals give up the will to survive because they believe they are going to die in the face of a severe threat to their survival. This has some similarity with humans who give up the will to keep going or keep trying because they believe they are going to fail anyway. When they do keep failing, they really do stop trying altogether. In different situations, they may give all the appearances of someone who is trying and cooperating but they believe 'What's the point? I'm going to fail' or 'it's not going to work for me anyway'. They do not persist; do not take chances with answers to questions. If they were to try, it would confirm what they already know – that it will be wrong *anyway*. Learned helpless individuals attribute failure to low ability and bad luck, and do not see any benefit in persistence and effort. They do not cause a lot of problems – they just do not start, or if they do, they present as depressed learners.

High self-worth concern

Individuals with this profile can be very challenging. When presented with an activity, it is met with *'I'm not doing this, it's rubbish,'* or *'It's below me,'* or *'I've done this before with someone else, I'm not doing it again,'* or they deliberately spoil sessions to avoid work. They can also be very selective in their cooperation with professionals, sometimes being cooperative with individuals who will not present tasks to them that undermine their self-worth. They keep most people at arm's length, and if anyone invades their protection of self (such as asking them to do something they fear they cannot do) they can be rude and abusive. Indeed, they prefer to be seen as rude, bolshy and abusive rather than having their ability called into question. Sometimes, the problems begin before a session starts, thus delaying the unwanted threat to self.

They often delay effort until an opportunity arises for them to demonstrate their ability. For example, there may have been a series of confrontations or unpleasant incidents, and then an activity provokes interest and the self does not feel threatened because they know they can do it. The task is done willingly, with effort and ability.

Self-determination

This is what we are aiming for. It enables the client to be intrinsically motivated towards presented activities. Self-determination is characterised by the 'flow experience,' i.e. all sense of time is lost because of being totally immersed in the activity.

Increasing motivation in learning

Help in overcoming learned helplessness

The chronic lack of persistence or not wanting to take any risks are the main symptoms of this style of motivation. Therefore, rewarding effort and persistence should be the main emphasis, i.e. a smile and a greeting for having made the effort for being there. A signal and/or attention for spending time on a task to reward persistence. What they produce is not important in the early stages – rewards are for being there and showing a little persistence.

The mutual use of *persistence graphs* can help highlight persistence and effort. At the end of a session both the client and professional provide an independent effort percentage. *'How hard do you think you tried in this session?'*

	%	%	%	%	%	%	%	%	%	%
Client	10	20	30	40	50	60	70	80	90	100

The client would draw a line to the percentage that they felt best represented the effort they had made in a session.

	%	%	%	%	%	%	%	%	%	%
Professional	10	20	30	40	50	60	70	80	90	100

Separately, the professional would do the same. Once both had completed their independent evaluation, they compare the percentages. They then discuss why they each gave that percentage, e.g. *'I gave myself 50% because I think I tried half the time.' 'Well I gave you 70% because although you tried half the time I think you took the risk of getting things wrong – you did not always play safe to stay comfortable. That is worth more.'*

The conversation should focus on the benefits of effort, persistence and taking risks. Percentage marks should be genuine, no favours given. It is the conversations about the marks that have been observed in practice as beneficial. It places 'effort' and 'persistence' as key areas of ability to develop. In Britain and USA, youth culture often derides effort. Frequently, it is seen as uncool to try – yet in other cultures (especially Asia) effort and persistence is perceived as an important aspect of skill and ability. Individuals can be taught the benefit of effort to performance.

The percentage marks can be converted into visual graphs – often, lists of percentage marks mean little to many. Seeing the result visually often helps to show how effort is, or is not, developing (see diagram 1.3).

Diagram 1.3: Persistence graph

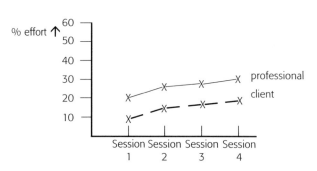

Remember – the shape of the graph, and the percentage marks are not that important. It is the end of sessions conversations that are important. Remember, too, the key words of 'effort', 'persistence', and conversations do not need to be lengthy. Do not use the approach for too long – a week or two is long enough.

A further method of helping learned helplessness individuals is to talk to them about it in more detail. This can be done in a group session, or individually. There could be discussions regarding how animals, when faced with a hopeless situation, close down and die, e.g. a dog whose owner has died, a rat whose brain relaxes when it cannot escape impending death and dies. Similar responses occur in humans, e.g. Sioux Indians, when they believed their function in life had finished would not die of starvation or exposure, but they would close down and die; married couples who often particularly in later years, die very soon after each other; individuals who die more quickly than expected when they discover they have a serious illness. We are capable of triggering learned helplessness to such a degree that we can seriously undermine our immune system and life survival skills. To be aware of this can help others tremendously.

Help in overcoming high self-worth concern

Those who want to maintain their high self-worth concern often have reputations to keep.

- It is essential not to be tempted into letting your emotions become engaged in conflict or aggression – individuals displaying this motivational style are very sensitive to displays of emotion that can trigger further responses.

- Stay neutral but firm, (this is where your three non-negotiables are useful, i.e. you can negotiate everything else but you stay firm on the three non-negotiables).

Protection of self-worth at all costs is the main symptom of this style of motivation. Therefore, to remove highly damaging threats to individuals regard to their perceived ability is the best alternative.

- **Do** compare performance on a task with the individual's previous attempt.

- **Do not** compare performance with other members of their training group (if you do, it is a little like saying *'You're not a bit like your brother/sister'*) – it becomes emotional.

- **Do** compare performance on a task with the average for their age group.

- **Do not** compare performance with the average in the training group.

Note: the method I use often for comparing an individual with their age range is to demonstrate it visually (see diagram 1.4).

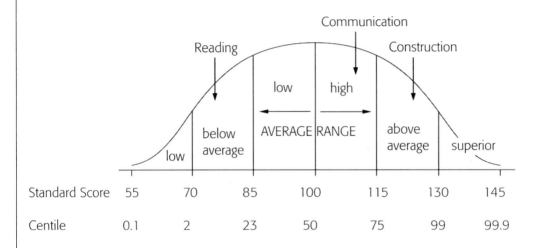

While looking at the shape (normal distribution curve), I will explain where their strengths and weaknesses are for their age group. I might say, *'Your reading skills may be here at the lowest 10% for your age range, but your communication skills are in the upper 35% and your construction skills are in the upper 10%'.* In other words, I present their skills and abilities as being *'all over the place – just like me'.* My DIY skills are in the lower 2%, my arithmetic skills are average, but my coping skills with crises are in the upper 20% (well, I like to believe it!). I am able to discuss with them multiple intelligences, i.e. that by a mixture of genes and experience we develop specific strengths and switch off other skills. Unfortunately, many areas of education and training do not encourage key areas of multiple intelligence, e.g. visual arts, creative movement, athletic prowess, social communication, design and building skills – and these are the areas that many of my clients have key strengths. It is those I accentuate, explain that schools often don't accentuate their key strengths, and then invite them to visit these opportunities and 'play' with them. Wherever possible, I will assess non-verbal abilities not usually assessed in education and training (basic literacy, numeracy and IT usually are), and demonstrate where they excel , are average, or not particularly strong. If assessment is not possible, it can be made from a series of visits to different visual/practical sites.

The key element is to demonstrate that intelligence is not fixed: it can change over time and sometimes is hidden or crushed because of lack of opportunity to express it.

- **Do** provide manageable challenges.

- **Do not** make the gap too large so that the individual suspects that feelings of incompetence are just around the corner.

Note: To achieve a feeling of competence, courses and schemes require step-by-step graduation of difficulty, as well as the eight motivational triggers mentioned earlier. I was once asked to observe a motor mechanics course at a college where one in three students left before the end of the first term, and only one in three remained at the end of the first year. While observing the practical elements of the course, I was impressed with the multi-sensory nature of the teaching (speaking, seeing, doing) the step-by-step approach, the challenge to try it yourself, etc – it was all working so well. The young trainees were engaged, and clearly benefiting from the learning experience. Subsequently, they moved onto the theory session – and I observed all hell breaking loose. For theorists keen to witness high self-worth concern kicking off – there it was for all to behold. Young men, with one or two young women, who had been previously biddable, became bolshy and often unmanageable. Those who didn't protect their self-worth this way, closed down their engagement, put their heads on the desk or quietly indicated they were going to the loo. I trailed around the workshop and looked at very large arch-lever files of worksheets packed with words and text. In my 25 years working in education and training, I have learned that the more practical a subject the more it will attract learners who are not great fans of the written word. They are more likely to have abilities in visual and practical skills. However, much of the training and education world still has a belief that to demonstrate your knowledge, you should be able to write about it. Some people cannot, rather than do not, i.e. they cannot represent their thoughts, feelings or knowledge on paper – but can in alternative forms of expression. Therefore, in motor mechanics, engineering, design, catering, multi-media – there will be more individuals with multiple intelligences high on one end of the practical/visual end of the continuum, with more weaknesses likely on the written expression side of the continuum.

Research in the late 1990s showed that 70–80% of students on art and design courses had dyslexic-type learning profiles (compared to a national rate of 4–10%). In our experience, 80% of trainees on motor mechanics courses have dyslexic-type problems. *So why ask them to demonstrate their knowledge on text-heavy worksheets?*

So, going back to the acting-out bolshy mechanics I was observing. They had moved from a style of learning they preferred and were comfortable with, to a theory, word-based session they were likely to find threatening, or had negative historical significance of classroom failure from school. Therefore, I requested access to all their NVQ files. All files were overwhelmingly bulky, packed with information that was word-based with few diagrams, pictures and charts. I asked a learning support assistant (LSA) to assess the files for readability levels – they were at an average reading age of 14–15 years, i.e. the same level as textbooks given to secondary school pupils at age 11 in Year 7 (perhaps this also explains many pupil's aggressive or passive response to reading – they can't read text at a level above their reading age). Many NVQ mechanics students were likely to have average reading levels well below this. Indeed, there is a simple readability formula that can reduce the difficulty of reading. Red banner tabloid newspapers use a similar formula, and hence maintain a high sales turnover.

I asked the LSA to address two main weaknesses of the NVQ files:

1. Reduce the readability level of the content of the files, and reduce the amount of wordage.

2. Increase the number of symbols, pictures and diagrams with one/two word explanations.

Discussion with lecturers further helped the LSA to know which key words should be maintained. These words were frequently included and often part of 'pick the right word for the box' in diagrams.

The reading formula I used was the Standard Measure of Gobbledegook (SMOG)*, i.e. a mathematical formula to simplify elaborated code to restricted code, i.e. crystal-clear English that gets to the point.

The new NVQ mechanics files now resemble picture books with brief wordage, and some lines or boxes on the page to answer short questions. The following academic year, the motor mechanics department reported that their retention rate of trainees had grown from 33% to 80%, with the majority of trainees achieving a merit or distinction.

What this demonstrates is that subject knowledge should not be primarily assessed by written answers – particularly if it is in practical or visual areas of study. St George's Hospital, London has appreciated this on its new medical course for doctors. Surprisingly, medical students entering the course with arts-based qualifications are doing better than their science-based peers – possibly because they are encouraged to be engaged in active learning, where they can use their existing knowledge to answer questions, *demonstrate* what they know, and not heavily rely on textbooks and written responses.

Finally, this type of approach is emphasising manageable challenges – and not making the learner believe that feelings of incompetence are just around the corner.

*See Appendix for further details

Motivational Triggers

Section 2
New pointers from research on motivation

By reviewing motivational research on a multi-cultural basis, effective international approaches to education and training can help guide future programmes.

Unfortunately, the UK model for educating young people frequently opposes the flow of motivation principles. John Barrett (2002), in his review of motivational principles and approaches, concluded that intrinsic motivation (doing something because you want to) is a substantially more powerful motivator than extrinsic motivation (doing something for a reward, or the expectation of an external reward). However, his analysis is a sad picture of what awaits most of our young people, i.e.:

- *Extrinsic motivation* – externally judged, tests, exams, sticks and carrots, performance indicators, stress, anxiety, competition...
  All these sabotage intrinsic motivation.

- *Intrinsic motivation* – internally judged, curiosity, enthusiasm, more time and effort, persistence, opportunity to finish the job...
  Promotes learning and creativity.

Approaches that promote intrinsic motivators are increasingly bearing successful outcomes. In USA, 70 charter schools are now based on motivational principles to learning. Barrett reports that retention and positive outcomes in these schools are consistently reaching the high ninety per cents. A popular approach in charter schools is for young people to attend school/college with a mentor who learns with the young person, i.e. they help each other to progress. Many of the mentors are retired, older members of the community. Both the learners use multi-media to help with their studies. When confusion, difficulty or misunderstandings occur, they can consult with a teacher (together or in a small group). Examinations are sat only by the young learner, when he/she believes that he/she is ready. This is done on a modular basis, sitting at a computer with immediate feedback on the result. The young person can then decide whether to 'cash in' that result, or opt to re-sit after further study.

The only reported problems, to date, in the charter schools are the difficulties meeting the large demand for multi-media programmes and the rate at which the learners are progressing through the schemes. Indeed, the opportunity of choice, regarding their route of training and education on a modular basis, is also seen as a key aspect of the success of the schools. Teachers are no longer perceived as crowd controllers in a classroom, but are professional consultants assisting a learning process when required. They remain busy, but are directly involved in assisting learning.

Thomas Telford Community College in Shropshire has adapted many of these principles, the first school in the UK to do so. Its success is increasingly well known. In recognition of his contribution, the school's principal recently received a knighthood – the first practising teacher to achieve such an accolade.

Conditions for effective learning

By short-handing the necessary conditions, we reach a raw and brief list of what is required for creating a motivational environment:

- relaxed

- learning and thinking are *fun*

- making connections between learning and real life

- question, guess, test approach

- value effort

- intrinsic motivation

- promote persistence in the face of obstacles

- seek new challenges.

Constraints for effective learning

Extrinsic motivators and performance indicators, e.g.:

- surveillance

- over-evaluation

- overcontrol

- deadlines

- unhelpful cultural beliefs.

Motivating the difficult to teach

Motivational styles that should be promoted or avoided:-

Adaptive	Maladaptive
task orientation	ego involvement resulting in work avoidance
success orientation	fear of failure of orientation
mastery orientation (Dweck, 2000)	learned helplessness: self-worth (Lombard, 1994; Covington, 1998; Dweck, 2000)

Motivational style is an outcome of interaction between *individuals* and *contexts*.

Thinking and rationality

Markman and Gentner (2000) investigated how young people's thinking affects rationality. To help change an individual's thinking significantly affects their level of rationality. Rationality is not static. *Active* processes can change an individual's level of rationality. This can best be achieved by helping an individual to be engaged in an educative process that:

- searches for solutions (as opposed to being told)

- searches for evidence (as opposed to being told)

- searches for verification (as opposed to being told)

- searces for more effective ways of presenting a new problem (as opposed to angry outbursts).

Irrationality = Giving up searching too soon, e.g. impulsiveness

They concluded that rationality is a continuum:

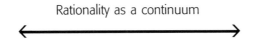

Rationality as a continuum

irrational	rational
less search	more search
impulsive	reflective
apathetic	enthusiastic
'autistic'	reality adjusted

Therefore, to aim for active searching processes is more likely to provoke intrinsic motivation, effective learning and increased rational thought.

Implications for schools/colleges/training providers

- learner-centred, not talk/chalk

- enablement, not controlled direction

- intrinsic motivation

- real feedback

- self-planning and self-monitoring

- regular workshops on learning, self-motivation, self-theories

- music and drama as the core programme.

Evidence of continued damage on educative process

Professor Galloway's (1998) review of UK schools found the following.

- The systematic ignoring of advice to government from teachers and research increases professional learned helplessness (not wanting to take risks, lack of persistence and effort).

- Dismissing genuine pupil achievements as misconceived also increases learned helplessness (why is it misconceived to learn without having tests?).

- Requiring schools to compete for pupils, funds and position in league tables results in:

  - reduction in mastery orientation in pupils and increases ego orientation (maladaptive motivational styles)

  - focusing on performance (which inhibits learning) which in turn promotes high self-worth orientation (pupils delaying effort, preferring to be seen as rude, bolshy and aggressive rather than not being able to perform or finish a task)

  - rejection of government policies.

Galloway posed the following question: 'Is pupil's motivation for schooling reduced by these effects on teachers' morale?'

Delinquency and diet

Gesch (2002) provided impressive evidence of the effects of diet on behaviour, particularly with regard to offending behaviour. He was able to demonstrate how unhealthy nutrition makes an important contribution to anti-social behaviour.

His study was carried out at HM Young Offenders Institution, Aylesbury. He worked with 230 young offenders – half were given a pill containing vitamins, minerals and essential fatty acids, and half were given a placebo. This was maintained over nine months. The baseline measure was the level of offences committed during the previous nine months before the trial began.

During the nine months of supplementation, compared with the placebo, the food supplement group committed:

- 25% fewer offences overall

- 40% fewer serious offences, especially violence.

In schools, we frequently ignore the effects of unhealthy food during the school day that inhibit performance, or of casually providing high-sugar vending machines selling cola and chocolate, which are known to have significant correlations with overactive, challenging and aggressive behaviours.

Ability *can* improve – but do we show how?

Rogoff (1999) has investigated the concept of 'thoughtless schooling'. He concluded that instead of students being taught *what* to think, we should be teaching them *how* to think. By being taught what to think, students do not see the relevance of what they are taught. The fear of failing degrades intellectual functioning because of the neglect of systematic teaching on *how* to think. Where this cognitive teaching occurs ability levels of young people improve.

Covington (1998) describes success and failure as psychological concepts. If individuals are free to choose their own goals they often minimise failure by lowering their *aspirations* (i.e. 'failure will lead to further failure, so I will choose things I can do'). If individuals exceed their chosen goals, they experience success, and thus raise aspirations, i.e. success breeds success.

To worry about failure leads to perceived inability, defensiveness, etc. Covington was able to demonstrate that success-oriented young people have guiding adults with high expectations, who provide strategy guidance on success and failure, reward persistence that leads to success, and ignore disappointing performances.

When the classroom becomes a competitive learning game, there is an inadequate supply of rewards (good grades) that are unequally distributed with the greatest number going to the best performers. For many, there are scarce rewards. Worse – learning becomes an ability game. Students begin to expend time and effort on avoiding losing and making others lose. Creativity, innovation, risk-taking and cooperation are lost. This type of competition in learning has been shown to lead to breakdown in personal integrity and destroys the love of learning.

Therefore, the ability game encourages the belief that some individuals are incapable of learning. Many young people go to school to learn how to fail. Schools become large bureaucracies where minorities and those disadvantaged disappear, never to be exposed to opportunities for knowledge and skills necessary for life beyond mere survival.

Covington (1998) recommends that schools, colleges and training providers begin to:

- teach how to play serious games with rules promoting motivational equity, strategic thinking, and reinforcing lessons learned from a failure

- teach serious games for preparing how to deal with the future (Loud Mouth Drama Group 2002* are superb advocates and demonstrators of this)

- teach serious games to enhance strategic thinking by moving knowledge away from recall of isolated facts and passing tests

- teach serious games to cope with young people's identities because game play becomes familiar with real-life situations

- teach serious games to demonstrate the value of knowledge, help job decisions and a place in the world of work

- provide simulations and apprenticeships – enablement, not preparation, should be the major aims

- have FIVE introductional guidelines:

  - provide engaging assignments

  - reward positive reasons for learning, e.g. relevant to their lives

  - put students in control

  - promote positive beliefs about ability

  - improve teacher-student relationships.

Motivational research is crystalising one clear finding over the last decade:

- competence, cooperation and sharing are the best indicators to predict future productivity

* Educational Theatre Company – Director: Eleanor Vale. www.loudmouth.fsbusiness.co.uk

- those who jostle to the top through high academic records driven by competitive motives are frequently counterproductive to later career success.

Is intelligence fixed or changeable?

Research in the last ten years clearly indicates that intelligence is changeable and not fixed (Gardner, 1993; Dweck, 2000; Barrett, 2002). Individuals that develop a self-theory of intelligence that believes ability is *fixed* (i.e. you are average, above average or below average and will remain that way), are more likely to have:

- a greater fear of failure

- performance goals (tests, exams) as measures of success

- the tendency to prevent themselves from seeking or taking learning opportunities

- higher depression scores than those who are not 'fixed' self theorists

- vulnerable personalities: they can become disorganised, defensive and helpless – they see failure as a lack of ability or low intelligence, and have a competitive view of education.

Individuals that develop a self-theory of intelligence that believes that ability is *incremental* (i.e. you can change your level of ability, knowledge, and intellectual understanding) are likely to:

- have an attitude of 'getting smarter'

- have learning goals, as opposed to performance goals

- have lower depression scores than fixed theorists – but even when incrementalists are depressed they maintain more active coping and effort

- thrive more than fixed theorists – emotionally, intellectually and in coping skills.

Once we adopt a self-theory of intelligence it affects what we value and how we approach intellectual tasks, how we interpret information, and how we respond to what happens to us.

Two clear pointers have recently emerged (Barrett, 2002).

1. Incremental self-theory can be taught to young people.

2. Do not praise for success on easy tasks – only for effort-dependent success.

Effort and ability

Asian cultures (including Australia) see effort as a major part of intelligence, much more so than UK or USA. Asians are incrementalists in their approach to learning. Their emphasis on effort is linked with the concept of malleable intelligence. Unfortunately, despite impressive classroom and instruction methods and achievement, there is often no emphasis on the love of learning and enjoyment of challenge. Instead, anxiety over grades and performance and pressure not to shame your family can lead to severe depression and humiliation over poor performance. Therefore, promotion of effort, the concept of the malleability of intelligence AND developing a love of learning are key factors.

Dweck (2000) asked a group of young people to supply percentages on how important they thought effort and intelligence were in relation to success. Results were:

- 'incremental self-theorists': intelligence = 65% effort, 35% ability

- 'fixed self-theorists': intelligence = 35% effort, 65% ability.

Further, for fixed theorists, effort was something to be avoided, or hidden, because it gives others a negative message about your ability. The majority of fixed theorists in the Dweck study engaged in a culture of extrinsic motivation, money as the primary reward, competition, short-termism.

Conversely, the incremental theorists saw effort as the key to achievement and self-esteem.

Laterality

Siegel (1999) proposed the laterality-attachment hypothesis. He investigated, and gained a large body of evidence, that right brains (right hemisphere) perceives the right brain output of another person. The right brain sends non-verbal communication via expressions, gestures and subsequently creates an image of the other's mind ('mindsight', or in Baron-Cohen's (2001) words 'theory of mind').

The left brain (left hemisphere) primarily sends out language-based communications. An adult, dismissive of the young person, will communicate with the young person mainly via the left hemisphere. The young person, attempting to avoid further communication with the adult, will also communicate mainly via the left hemisphere.

Siegel recommends that experiences to integrate left and right hemispheres may improve personal and interpersonal lives. He recommends:

- interpersonal and personal training for teachers and pupils

- promotes the need for narratives and stories – young and old sharing stories, thus influencing and creating both mental *and* neural organisation.

Siegel goes on to explain that when minds connect there is a feeling of exhilaration, immediacy, clarity and authenticity ('flow'). Such heightened moments of engagement lead to an appreciation of power relationships that can help nurture and heal.

These findings add weight to the approach of promoting creative and innovative activities that are right-brain-based, e.g. visual and practical. Also, that teaching young people non-verbal skills through personal and social activities has additional benefits. Again, drama and music are useful vehicles to promote right-brain activity.

Finally, Siegel explains that left-brain to left-brain communications produce shared attention to objects. Right-brain to right-brain communications produce shared attention to emotion. The ideal is to integrate left and right hemispheres to improve lives, learning and relationships.

Teenagers – friends and families

Coleman and Hendry (1999) conducted a long and detailed look at the nature of adolescence in families and peer groups. Several clear findings emerged from their research:

- teenage peer groups are not in opposition to parental values

- both are often complementary: peers for fashion, parents for education, careers and morality

- teenagers very frequently choose friends with similar views to parents, but often *deny* this

- friends and peer groups are important to develop social skills, social support, popularity and status (dress, music, leisure, opinions)

- this conformity for dress, music, etc reduces as self-confidence increases

- loneliness in teenagers requires special attention

- adults need to involve teenagers in group processes in a more genuine and open way

- adolescence should be viewed as a longer process now, e.g. 9–21 years of age

- continuing connectedness with parents is helpful for transition into adulthood.

This latter point was further confirmed in research from the Family Conference, London, 2002. A young person requires to 'connect' with only one parent to progress in this type of transition. Adams (2003) examines some of these issues, while Coleman and Roker (2001) provide a handbook on the parenting of teenagers including the issues of youth crime, working with fathers as well as mothers of teenagers, and working with ethnic minorities. It addresses the practical issues of how to assess parents and what kind of support to provide.

Finally, Coleman and Hendry (1999) emphasise the need to teach social skills to help teenagers avoid offending. Other work has discovered that some social phobias are directly related to weak social skills. Often these can be taught using a variety of non-verbal communication skills exercises (Streng and Searle, 1996; Nowicki, 2000 and Lombard, 2003). These issues will be discussed in another publication by Lombard entitled 'Social Competence.'

Conclusion

This final section on new research in motivation is intended as a guide for future reading, a direction for those who are studying higher degrees while working with young people, and providing an indicator of the future direction of this type of work. Any other new and exciting approaches or texts would be gratefully received by the author.

Motivational Triggers

References

Abramson, L.E., Seligman, M.E.P. & Gardner, J. (1980), *Learned Helplessness in Humans: An Attributional Analysis*, in J. Gardner and M.E.P. Seligman (Eds) *Human Helplessness*, New York: Academic Press.

Adams, G. and Berzonsky, M. (2003), *Handbook of Adolescence*, Oxford: Blackwell.

Baron-Cohen, S. (2001), *The Reading the Mind in the Eyes Test*, Revised Version, Journal of Child Psychology and Psychiatry, **42**, 2, 241–251.

Barrett, J.H.W. (2002), *Motivating Disaffected Teenagers*, a series of 52 lectures in The Lifelong Learning and Public Programmes, University of Bristol's Department of Psychology.

Coleman, J. and Hendry, L.B. (1999), *The Nature of Adolescence*, London: Routledge.

Coleman, J. and Roker, D. (2001), *The Parenting of Teenagers*, London: Jessica Kingsley.

Covington, M. (1998), *The Will to Learn: A Guide for Motivating Young People*. Cambridge: Cambridge University Press.

Covington, M.V. & Beery, R.G. (1976), *Self-Worth and School Learning*, New York: Holt, Rinehart & Winston.

Covington, M.V. (1984), *The motive for self-worth* in C. Ames and R.E. Ames (Eds) *Research on Motivation in Education* (Volume 1), London: Academic Press.

Craske, M.L. (1988), *Learned Helplessness, Self-Worth Motivation and Attribution Re-training for Primary School Children*, British Journal of Educational Psychology, **58**, 152–164.

Dweck, C.S. (2000), *Self-Theories: Their Role in Motivation, Personality and Development*, Hove: Psychology Press.

Emler, N. & Reicher, M. (1995), *Adolescence & Deliquency*, Oxford: Blackwell.

Galloway, D. (1998), *Motivating the Difficult to Teach*, Harlow: Longman.

Galloway, D. & Rodgers, C. (1989), *Disruptive Behaviour, Effective Schooling and Motivational Style,* paper for NAPCE/NACRO seminar on juvenile crime, Wolverhampton.

Gardner, H. (1993), *The Unschooled Mind*, London: Harper Collins.

Gesch, C.B. (2002), *Delinquency and Diet*, British Journal of Psychiatry, **181**, 1.

Lombard, G.F. (1992), *Enhancing Adolescents' Self Efficacy*, PhD Thesis, University of Bristol.

Lombard, G.F. (1994), *Disturbing Pupils' Perceptions of Motivational Deficits*, Educational and Child Psychology, **11**, 2, 39–47.

Lombard, G.F. (2003), *Social Competence: reading other people*, Trowbridge: Lifetime Careers Publishing.

Markman, A.B. and Gentner, D. (2002), *Thinking and Rationality*, Annual Review of Psychology, **52**, 223–247.

Maslow, A. (1968), *Toward a Psychology of Being*, New York: Van Nostrand.

Nowicki, S. (2000), *DANVA 2*, Atlanta, USA: Dyssemia Inc.

Rogoff, B. (1999), *Everyday Cognition: Its Development in Social Context*, iuniverse.com

Seligman, M.E.P. (1975), *Helplessness: On Depression, Development and Death*, San Francisco: Freeman.

Siegel, D.J. (1999), *The Developing Mind: Neurobiology of Interpersonal Experience*, London: Guilford Publishers.

Streng, I. and Searle, G. (1996), *The Social Skills Game*, London: Jessica Kingsley.

Appendix

SMOG readability formula – simplified

Readability is an attempt to match the reading level of written material to the 'reading with understanding' level of the reader.

This formula calculates readability using sentence and word length. However, other factors affect understanding of what you are reading that cannot be measured in this way, e.g. motivation of reader, size and type of print, layout of written material, previous knowledge of subject, style of writer, etc.

SMOG is much quicker and easier to work out by hand than other formulae.

1. select a text

2. count 10 sentences

3. count number of words which have three or more syllables

4. multiply this by 3

5. circle the number closest to your answer

    1 4 9 16 25 36 49 64 81 100 121 144 169

6.   find the square root of the number you circled

1 4 9 16 25 36 49 64 81 100 121 144 169
1 2 3 4 5 6 7 8 9 10 11   12 13

7.   Add 8.

A readability level under about 10 will be able to be understood by most people.

Once you master SMOG with a bit of practice, you realise that short, regular words serve just as well as long, multi-syllable irregular words. For example:

Question: What does this mean: '*Assess and critically evaluate the brown, viscous liquid contained in the glass receptacle*'?

Answer: It means: '*How's your pint?*'

The first way the question is worded is in elaborated code, used in textbooks and examination questions. The alternative question '*How's your pint?*' is in restricted code usually used in relaxed conversation between relatives and friends. It is the restricted code (linked with visual images) I promote for practical areas of study and training.